Crawdad Creek

By Scott Russell Sanders

Illustrated by Robert Hynes

NATIONAL GEOGRAPHIC SOCIETY

Washington, D.C.

Text copyright © 1999 Scott Russell Sanders

Illustrations copyright © 1999 Robert Hynes
To create his artwork Robert Hynes used acrylics in a watercolor technique on vellum bristol board.

Published by the National Geographic Society
1145 17th Street N.W.
Washington, D.C. 20036-4688

Library of Congress Cataloging-in-Publication Data
Sanders, Scott R. (Scott Russell), 1945–
Crawdad Creek / by Scott Russell Sanders ; illustrated by Robert Hynes.
p. cm
Summary: Two children find fossils, salamanders, dragonflies, frogs, deer tracks,
and many other "treasures" when they visit the creek near their home.
ISBN 0-7922-7097-5
[1. River ecology—Fiction. 2. Brothers and sisters—Fiction.]
I. Hynes, Robert, ill. II. Title.
PZ7.S19786Cr   1999
[E]—dc21   98-25163

The world's largest nonprofit scientific and educational organization, the National Geographic Society was
founded in 1888 "for the increase and diffusion of geographic knowledge." Since then it has supported
scientific exploration and spread information to its more than nine million members worldwide.

The National Geographic Society educates and inspires millions every day through magazines, books,
television programs, videos, maps and atlases, research grants, the National Geography Bee,
teacher workshops, and innovative classroom materials.

The Society is supported through membership dues and income from the sale of its educational products.
Members receive NATIONAL GEOGRAPHIC magazine—the Society's official journal—discounts
on Society products, and other benefits.

For more information about the National Geographic Society and its educational programs and
publications, please call 1-800-NGS-LINE (647-5463) or write to the following address:
National Geographic Society
1145 17th Street N.W.
Washington, D.C. 20036-4688

Visit the Society's Web site:
www.nationalgeographic.com

Printed in U.S.A.

For Anna and Liam Lane-Zucker
—S.R.S.

For Bryan, Ben, and Anna
—R.H.

THE CREEK behind our house talks all the time. It whispers in the hot months when the water is low, and it murmurs in the cold months under a skin of ice. After snow melts or rain falls, the creek nearly shouts.

What does it say? I couldn't tell you, any more than I could tell you what the frogs are saying when they croak or the birds when they sing or the winds when they rustle the trees. I just love to listen.

So I'm always glad to visit the creek, especially in the summer when the air is like an oven.

One muggy day, my little brother Michael and I decided to go down to the creek and pan for gold. Dad gave us a shovel for digging up gravel. Mom gave us two cake pans for dipping water and swishing the gravel around. We dipped, we swished, hunting for nuggets in our tin pans, and we talked about how we'd spend our money once we struck it rich.

"Look here, Lizzie!" he would cry, or "Look here, Mike!" I would cry, whenever we thought we'd spied some gold. But it always turned out to be a shiny pebble or a bit of yellow leaf.

What we did find were
fossils—the curvy outlines of shells,
the feathery shapes of ferns, even
the slinky tunnels of worms.

Mom told us our fossils were millions of years old. Just think! After all those millions of years, we could still dig up worms in the mud, see ferns curling on the banks, and find mussels hunched in their shells down on the bottom of the creek.

Once Michael found an arrowhead in the gravel, and he called me
to come see. It was a beauty, made
from stone the color of chocolate,
as long as my thumb, sharp enough
so we handled it carefully. The people
who'd chipped the arrowhead, Mom
told us, had lived here hundreds of
years ago—maybe even thousands.

I wondered if those long-ago
people had ever stood here listening
to water burble over rocks.

Pretty soon we forgot about panning for gold, there were so many other treasures in the creek. Turn over a rock, for instance, and you might find a salamander, all rosy and quick. Turn over a rock, and you were almost sure to find a crayfish, all jerky and pale, with its eyes peering around on stalks and its claws clicking.

"Now that's a mean-looking crawdad," our own dad said when we showed him one.

So that's how we got the name Crawdad Creek.

There was life everywhere we looked.
Snails grazed over mossy rocks, hauling their
houses on their backs. Dragonflies zipped from
shore to shore. In quiet pools, water striders
skittered around on their six bent legs, making
bright dimples on the surface with their feet.

Turtles lined up on logs to soak in
the sun, like green bowls laid out to dry.
Every now and again, a snake swam down
the middle of the creek, with its head
plowing a straight line through the water
and its body rippling behind
like a flag in the breeze.

No matter how many times Michael and I
visited the creek, the frogs always sounded surprised.
Crackittty! they hollered, then plopped into the water.

Fish jumped, too, nabbing at bugs, then fell back
in with a splash. Silver minnows darted through the
shallows. Deeper down, whiskery catfish loafed,
their big tails fanning.

We described what we saw to Mom and Dad, and they told us the names of everything, or else they helped us look up the names in books.

So we discovered the name of the kingfisher, a fat blue-and-white bird that liked to perch on a dead limb over the creek, then swoop down and gobble minnows. We discovered the names of whirligig beetles and damselflies and critters so small we had to spy them with a magnifying glass.

Dad taught us to recognize the tracks that animals had left in the mud. We learned the five-toed print from the paw of a raccoon, the two pointy holes from the hoof of a deer, the spiky marks of a crow, even the tiny scratches of a mouse.

"And those," Dad said, pointing at our own barefoot prints in the mud, "are Michael and Elizabeth tracks."

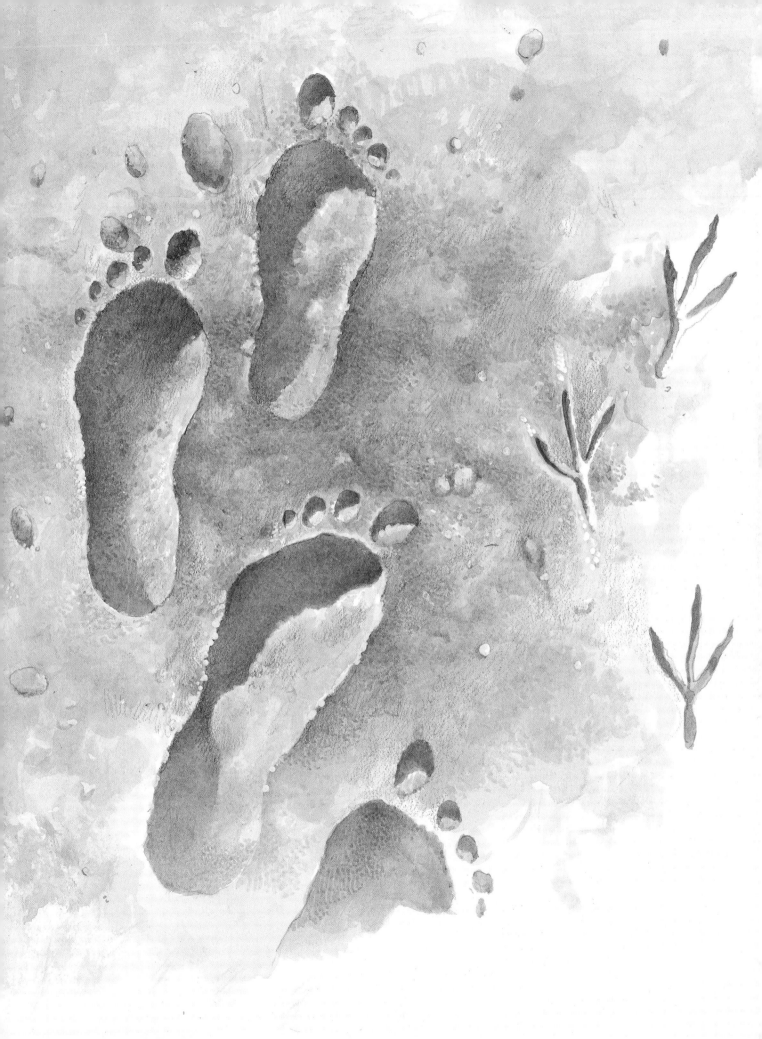

In the warm evenings, just before
going in to bed, we sat very still beside
Crawdad Creek, hoping to see the animals
that made the tracks. And sure enough,
we saw deer coming down to drink, saw
rabbits nibbling and muskrats swimming,
even saw raccoons grubbing for mussels
in the water.

When the weather turned too cool for wading, Michael and I put the shovel back in the garage and the cake pans back in the kitchen. We never found any gold, at least not the kind you wear on a ring around your finger. But I felt rich all the same.

Cold weather or hot, I still go down to the creek every chance I get. There's always something to see. In daylight, the water glows with all the colors of the sky.

One morning, a sycamore leaf came floating by, the sides curled up to form a little boat, and there inside, as calm as you please, sat a butterfly. While I watched, the butterfly opened its orange-and-black wings, and flew.

On clear nights before the moon comes up, stars waver on the surface like fireflies. Wind ruffles the water like a hand brushing over silky cloth.

In the morning before I go to school and at night before I go to bed, I can hear the mutter and mumble of water pouring over rocks. Even when there are no other critters in sight, I'm never lonesome at Crawdad Creek, because the water keeps talking.

A NOTE FROM THE AUTHOR

I spent much of my childhood outside, exploring the woods and fields, turning over rocks, lying in the grass to watch clouds or stars, tracking deer, peering at flowers and bugs, drinking in through all my senses the living, breathing world. My parents put up with my questions. They encouraged my curiosity, let me ramble and look to my heart's content. We didn't own a television until I was nearly a teenager, and even then, little was broadcast over the few channels of our black-and-white set that would hold my attention. There were no computers to distract me, no video games, no battery-powered gizmos. I loved to read, but I could do that sitting in the shade of a tree or beside a creek.

My favorite creek as a boy, and the one I had chiefly in mind as I wrote this book, ran through the woods behind our house in Ohio. But I've been mesmerized by hundreds of creeks in dozens of states, by rivers and brooks and gutters running with rain. I love all moving water. My favorite companion on those early visits to creeks, and the person I thought of as I imagined the character of Elizabeth, was my sister, Sandra, who's older than I am by four years, a keen observer and a patient soul. She also tolerated my endless questions. She kept me from harm. Once, when I foolishly tried to balance on a log in a flooded river, she saved my life.

I feel blessed from having spent so much of my childhood outdoors. I wrote about Elizabeth and Michael's adventures on Crawdad Creek in hopes of inviting today's children to go outside, hunt for moving water, open their eyes and ears and hearts to the wildness that wells up everywhere.

—Scott Russell Sanders
Bloomington, Indiana